Get Customers and Keep Them!

Step by Step Guide to Target Marketing

Susan Kilmer

Table of Contents

Introduction

I wanted to start off by thanking you (the reader) for taking an interest in my guide. The main purpose of writing this brief guide is to help both the aspiring entrepreneur and seasoned business owner alike better understand how to attract new customers and retain current customers regardless of what your business is; the principles are the same.

The sole purpose of any business is to sell to their core group of customers at the right price, right place and at the right time. If this doesn't happen, a business will never get a potential customer to buy. All businesses have to appeal to the potential customer and <u>not</u> convince them to buy.

My goal for this brief guide is for the reader to better understand the basics of marketing and consumer behavior, so that you can operate your businesses better and generate more potential revenue.

Enjoy!

For those of you who purchased this book because you also wanted free access to the bonus material, please click here to access it for free now!

To subscribe to the ***Marketing by Susan Tips and Tricks*** at for free information about how to get customers, marketing strategies and other tips and tricks, opt in here

Chapter 1: What is Marketing?

A big problem that business owners face is that they do not market consistently but rather do so when there is an awareness of a decline in or nonexistent sales. Another problem is business owners tend to market without a clear objective or goal.

According to the dictionary, marketing is the process of promoting, selling, and distributing a product or service to potential buyers, consumers and end users. Marketing is also simply actions such promoting, telling, showing, offering or developing products and/or services to potential customers. Small businesses have limited resources for marketing and do not have access to media coverage, ad placement, tradeshows and other channels to reach as many people to build enough awareness for the opportunity to sell.

Marketing **ESPECIALLY** means to business owners is understanding that a person can have the best product or service in the world but if you cannot get the right customers at the right price, at the right time your business will not survive.

So who are your customers?

EVERYBODY!!!

WRONG. If you are selling to everyone, you are technically selling to no one. It is physically and financially impossible to everyone because everyone's needs are different. You may be thinking, so what? Consumer behavior is the process to which a consumer uses to choose and consume a product or service. Although it is partially a conscious act, the products or services we do purchase is based on an accumulation of all of our needs, wants and environmental influences since birth. Understanding consumer behavior is a science that most business owners do not truly understand and the best way to offset that lack of skill is to be aware of potential customers' needs and wants, simply by asking them about it. You want to especially focus on your **target customers (market).**

Why perform marketing actions?

Without building an awareness of what your business has to sell and why it will benefit target customers, people simple will not buy because they will not know that your business exists. Simply throwing a business out there isn't enough to make someone want to buy from you. You can't make a person buy something and even if you did, they'd never become a loyal customer because the experience wasn't out of free will.

For a business to succeed, the business and its products or services must be known to potential customers. Unless your business is well known and you often communicate with them, you will have to use marketing strategies to create brand awareness.

When are you marketing?

Marketing is an activity within your business that encompasses everything within and outside of your business. It involves looking at what you are doing within your business and what is happening around it so you should always be marketing.

Marketing is what you do with print and outdoor ads, radio, television, email campaigns and social media.

Marketing also means much more. It also means what you and your employees do and say to customers, on your marketing materials, website, what your office space looks like, any vehicles you drive and how you drive them. It also means any of your business partners, how your other customers behave and also any future successes and failures you have.

All of these aspects within your business is essentially components of marketing because all of those actions build a perception the world has about your business and what your business is about.

Build Your Brand

It takes very little and a short amount of time for perception to be built of your business so you should very quickly before the start of your business and even at the start, build a brand about your business that you want potential and current customers to perceive about your business and all of your business activity and attitudes need to encompass that brand. You have the choice and the opportunity at all times especially at the start where it is greatest to control the perception people will have about your business.

All of these activities create and shape your business image so what do you want to be known for vs. how customers may perceive you. Is it quality, fast service, cleanliness, professional or a low price leader?

In the next chapter, we will talk about how to start the process of the basics of marketing and identifying the right customers for your business which will increase the chances you have of building the right brand you need and should be known for.

Chapter 2: Product and Service Definition

You begin the process of target marketing by taking a look at the products and services you would like to sell. Every single product or service should be a solution to a problem, fulfill a need or improve an existing solution not based on simply a want. Sustainability cannot exist without true value offered that exists beyond wants and features.

Start by listing and describing each of your products or services including its' attributes, features, benefits and know what purpose each item serves in solving a target customer's needs. The questions you need to be asking yourself is:

* What are your products and services' features?
* What benefits do they provide?
* What are the benefits of the benefits

Remember, customers only buy products for **end user benefits** of a product or service features and not the features itself!

Think about all of the smart phones out there, especially the most popular one. You know which one I am referring to but in thinking about this particular brand and all of its reoccurring customers, what is it perceived as? Think beyond functionality:

a. Personal Assistant/Organizer
b. Device that keeps you connected with loved ones
c. Fitting In/Ego
d. Other
e. All of the above

The answer is **C. Fitting In / Ego**. The reasoning behind this answer is there are hundreds of smart phone brands out there that can do the same things: be a personal assistant/organizer, allows you to call/email/text loved ones, etc. but the difference between these brands and the most popular brand is that the 14-25 year old target market (core group of customers) buy based on what is most popular in itself because they themselves want to belong.

The next step is to identify who has the needs that match your benefits. When trying to identify who to sell to and how to market, you start with a systematic process before you go out and market to potential customers. In each of the following chapters, we will go into more depth about each step in the process of reaching and selling effectively to your target market:

* Product and Service Differentiation
* Identify Value Proposition / Unique Selling Proposition

- Create a Profile of the Target Market
- Analyze Target Market's Demand
- Analyze Competition
- Evaluate Choices
- Create Targeted Messaging and Effective Marketing Campaign
- Create Branding
- Identify Proper Channels
- Tracking and Marketing Analysis

Chapter 3: What is a Target Market?

A target customer or target market is a specific, core group of people to which a business sells its products and/or services. Your target market is your ideal client that will be responsible for most of your potential revenue. If you do not focus on meeting your target market's needs, you never sell enough to cover your expenses and will missing out any potential revenue. Selling to a focused group of people is not only easier but also more cost efficient.

Selling to other businesses requires a different strategy than selling to consumers. If you are selling to other businesses, you need to understand that their main concern is how your product will or service help them increase profits. When you are selling to a consumer, you need to understand that their main concern is how your product will or service benefit them. Your target market is about who is **REALLY** going to buy what you have to sell.

When selling a product and/or service, you need to take the entire population of who you could potentially sell to and breaking down that group into a specialized segment who will be the most likely buy what you have to sell. If you take two women, both 25-40 years old, same ethnicity but have different lifestyles such as a soccer mom vs a working professional, would you sell to these two women in the same way?

Of course not. Each woman, although from the same neighborhood, same age, same education and income levels do not exactly have the same lifestyles and thus their needs for what you have to sell may be different. If you owned a fast food restaurant chain, the young professional more than likely would purchase coffee and thus speed is a big factor for why they would buy and the soccer mom would care more about if you have something that would appeal to her kids but it has a kid friendly environment.

As a result you cannot sell to both women the same. Unfortunately, there are hundreds if not thousands (and maybe even more than that) different kinds of lifestyles for women of the same age demographic as we described. So how can you appeal to them all? You can't. Which is why it is necessary to be a little more targeted and segmented.

Thus target marketing is breaking a market into segments and then focusing your efforts on one or a few segments. A lot of the household detergent companies do this with their different products and aim their individualized marketing messages to those specific target markets. For instance, some of their products are aimed at mothers to keep cleaned baby clothes safe and soft.

One key way to better understand your target market is by starting with creating a definition of that target market's characteristics by dividing them into different segmented categories such as: **behavioral, demographic, geographic, psychographic etc.**

Demographic segmentation is thinking about the profile of your customers by looking at aspects such as their age, gender, location, income level, social class, occupation, education and marital status if they are a consumer buyer. If you are selling to a business you want to think about their industry, their location, size of firm, quality, technology used and price preferences.

Psychographic segmentation is thinking about what do customers think about, what they value by looking at how they live including their lifestyle, hobbies and interests.

Behavioral segmentation is thinking about what benefits do the customers want by looking how do and will they use the product or service

Geographic segmentation is thinking about where does the customer live and how can they be reached.

Looking at also the buying stage of the customer will determine how likely they are to be from you. Customers at the early stage are speculative about what you have to sell versus customers who are already convinced are more likely to be easily influenced.

When profiling the customer, you will need to ask yourself several questions:

- Why do they buy?
- Where do they buy?
- When do they buy?
- What are they willing to pay?
- What do they care about?
- Why will they come back?

Then tailor your marketing strategies to the answers to these questions.

Think about the scenario we referenced earlier:

Two 25-40 year old women, both living in an upper class neighborhood with the same income, education, ethnicity but two different lifestyles: Soccer Mom vs. Business Professional.

When it comes to most products that they will purchase, will they acquire the same things around the same days, times, hours and quantities? More likely not. Although both women have similar profiles, their lifestyles are different.

Lifestyles impact when they do things, what they are interested in and what their priorities are so as a business owner we can assume we can't target and sell to everyone because it is physically and financially impossible to do so.

So instead of trying to assume the entire population will be interested in what you have to sell, it is far easier to figure out who would naturally be interested in the types of things you have to sell, understand their characteristics and where they typically are at, and communicate with them in ways they understand. This is far easier than trying to convince people to buy from you.

The **SOLE** existence of your business is to provide your core group of customers with the products/services they need, at the price they expect in the areas/times that they want.

REMEMBER the 80/20 Rule:
"20% of customers contribute to 80% of your sales"
(target customers)

The second goal of your business is to service your core group of customers (target market) well enough so that they become loyal customers. Loyal customers are very important because they are:

- Less sensitive to price changes
- They provide word-of-mouth and referrals
- Likely to purchase multiple or supplemental products/services
- Require less educating and selling time
- Makes your job easier and more satisfying

Knowing these facts about your potential target market will enable you to better shape your business strategies and operations in meeting their needs. It will also help shape your elevator pitch and messaging on all of your marketing material and website.

Chapter 4: Know Your Competition

Knowing your competition is another important aspect of getting and keeping customers. If you become more aware of who your competitors are, you become aware of what influencing your business externally and how well your business will continue to do. It isn't simply enough to just focus on what you do within your business, but you have to be aware of what is going on around your business.

One way you can do this is by paying attention to your competition. Your competition are operating their business day to day finding inventive ways to earn more revenue and more customers and more market share in your industry. You can choose to not pay attention to what is happening to your business' external environment but your competition isn't ignoring it and it is just enough to take any potential customers you may have had a chance at getting.

Consumers do not care at who you are as a person nor do they care about the cause or your passion unfortunately. Even loyal customers can be swayed if what is important to them is affected. This will always be how it is, so the sooner you understand that you have to constantly meet your current customers' needs always and finding ways to bring in new customers you will stay in business.

When you are analyzing your competition you need to be aware of everything about their business as much as you know about your business. To get started, until you develop systems and processes, be aware of:

- What your competition does well and what does it do not so well
- How they price their products
- Which target markets are they currently selling to
- How they are branding their business
- Where are they currently selling
- What their current customers think about them

You will utilize all of these aspects of your competitors to not only capitalize on their weak points but also gauge where you are weak in and where you need to improve.

Chapter 5: Analyze your Communication Strategies

Whether you are in business or not in business yet, you need to take a look at the strategies you have built up in your business or the strategies you designed that you would like to implement once you are in business and you will need to evaluate your choices:

- Will your target market understand your product or service's benefit(s) that will be provided to them?

- Do you understand thoroughly what influences your target market to make decisions on what, where, when and why they buy?

- Can your target market actually afford your pricing?

- Can you reach your target market with your messaging?

Also ask yourself:

- Will you get or are you getting in front of the right customers?

- Will you get or are you getting in front of enough of the right customers?

- Do you have a message that will clearly communicate the values and brand of your business?

- For those of you that are already in business, are your strategies getting the desired outcomes when you are in front of your customers or are you not in front of the right customers still?

You should also ask yourself if your business message:

- Accurately communicates the products or services of your company

- Communicates the attributes and benefits of your products or services of your company

- Communicates the value of your business versus your competitors

- Meets the individual customers' expectations. Remember you are services the individual but marketing to groups.

There are major goals you will want your business to achieve in order to be successful, but first you must invest time into defining your target customer, developing the right message to bring them in and then identifying the most marketing methods to reach them.

An effective marketing strategy and campaign is a campaign that has:

- A clear product and/or service

- Defined customers

- Targeted message

- Consistent branding

- Appropriate channels and

- Thorough tracking and evaluation method.

Chapter 6: Branding and Messaging

So what is branding and messaging anyway? Branding is a comprehensive experience for your customers and their perception of your business. For branding to be effective it must be consistent every time so that your customers will know what to expect.

Branding is all encompassing as well. It includes your logo, style, design or look, interactions, voice, tone, content of message etc.

Messaging is also a part of branding. Messaging is essentially what it is you want your customer to know about your business. Your message must clearly communicate and support your business' objectives and goals, your messaging must support your customer's point of view and preferences and it needs to be useful info most of the time and sales pitches the rest of the time. Remember potential customers need to know, trust and like you before they will buy from you often enough or buy from you at all.

Chapter 7: Sample Marketing Problems and Strategies to Combat Them

Marketing Problem #1: It is more expensive and tough get new customers to buy enough to keep you in business.

Fact: It is more expensive to get new customers than it is to keep an existing one. In most cases, most of your profits will come from a core group of your customers (target market).

Solution: Some solutions and strategies could be tactics such as providing discounts to your most valued customers, develop a loyalty program with product or monetary rewards for repeat purchases or give a thoughtful reward or surprise to your best customers.

Marketing Problem #2: Most customers like your product or services but do not always know the best way to provide word of mouth or do not do it at all.

Fact: Customers can easily forget to mention your product or service in their daily life unless they are reminded of it.

Solution: Some solutions and strategies could be tactics such as asking your customers to refer you, providing customers with marketing material such as your business card or promotional items to pass on or simply knowing your sales pitch and find subtle ways to insert it into normal conversations with your customers or potential customers.

No Cost to Low Cost Marketing Strategies

- Be active on the right social media sites that your target customer is on. Keep in mind that social media will never bring you sales, it is a long term strategy to maintain an existing brand. But first you must build a brand outside of social media.

- Become an expert in your field and do everything you can to make sure your target customers know it and believe it

- Blog on your website and other websites to maximize your exposure to the right potential customers

- Build your email list with quality names

- Create a vlogging channel online

- Offer your potential customers and visitors to your website a freebie or give away or write an e-book such as the one you are reading right now and self-publish.

- You can also let your loyal customers review your business and incorporate their reviews on your websites and blogs and testimonials.

- However, not all exposure has to be just online, you need to make yourself the expert in your field out in the local community. You can also form a group that can provide something of value to the marketplace in which you specialize.

- You can also become known as an expert and obtain potential customers (other businesses) at trade associations for your industry or at chambers of commerce networking events especially if you are a service based business that provides services to other businesses such as web development, bookkeeping/accounting, graphic design or any other service another business will need use.

THE END.

I wanted to thank all of you for taking the time to read this beginner's guide to marketing. I do hope it gave you a clear explanation of what marketing is, why it is important, what is a target market (customer), what is the most important pieces of knowing who they are, knowing who your competitor is and how all of these aspects help you build your business to sell more.

I hope you have enjoyed the book and if you could take the time and review the book. Reviews help me become aware of what you enjoyed and didn't enjoy within the book and what you would like for me to improve. It also will help me find out about what other information you will want to know in the future.

For those of you who want to review the book, you can do so by clicking here.

Thank you.

For those of you who purchased this book because you also wanted free access to the **bonus books**, please click here to access it for free now!

To subscribe to the *Marketing by Susan Tips and Tricks* at for free information about how to get customers, marketing strategies and other tips and tricks, opt in here

Starting a Small Business
(BONUS BOOK)

Easy How to Guide to Starting a Business Successfully

Susan Kilmer

Table of Contents

Introduction

I wanted to start off by thanking all of you, the readers, for taking an interest in **Starting a Home Business: A Step-By-Step Guide.** The main purpose of writing this guide is to assist both aspiring entrepreneurs and new business owners alike better understand the proper preparation, planning and start-up process of any business venture they would like to pursue.

Studies show that the average small business shuts down within 3-5 years for a variety reasons and certain industries especially such as the food and beverage industry shuts down typically within a couple of years but very few business owners truly understand what exactly led to their closure.

Most attribute it to lack of a customer base, which is a common reason but it is primarily because a lot of the problems that did occur were due to mistakes being made prior to the business being open and the business owner did not start the business properly and implement the correct systems and infrastructure from the beginning.

My goal for this guide is for the readers such as yourself, who do decide to purchase and read this book, to better understand the fundamentals and basics of starting a business and how to navigate through this seemingly difficult process.

Enjoy!

For those of you who purchased this book because you also wanted free access to the **bonus books**, please click here to access it for free now!

If you would like to subscribe to the *Starting a Business by Susan Monthly Tips and Tricks* newsletter for **FREE** information about how to start, grow and operate your business more successful, you can subscribe and opt-in here.

Chapter 1: Misconceptions and False Assumptions about Owning a Small Business

When individuals decide to start a small business or any business venture most often they start the process with assumptions ingrained in their brain about what the business environment is like without truly questioning what they hear or read. Having a belief without documented proof and research to backup that belief often leads the aspiring entrepreneur to make decisions and create strategies for their business that often times is completely wrong for their business and they are left wondering what happened.

I wanted to start off this book before we move on to the nitty gritty, listing out some of the common false beliefs people often have that typically lead to a lot of risks along the way. My hope is that if you or anyone who has any, some or all of these assumptions and beliefs listed below, that you have the capacity to change your mindset from assuming/believing to actually *knowing*. Also, that you learn to research everything you hear or read and make a well thought out decision before you take any action regarding the needs of your business.

Some common <u>false assumptions and strategies</u> are:

1. **Relying heavily on others for answers and information without question**.

   Do not believe everything you read and hear. Instead, get into the habit of researching information and knowledge you obtain from others and understand **WHY** and *"connect the dots"* between facts and concepts. If you do not know why situations and facts are the way they are, then you will not have the ability to critically think through every situation you will come across in the life span of your business. If you have a business and you find yourself unsure of what you should be doing, why people aren't buying or you are standing there twiddling your thumbs confused, then you either have done something wrong, do not talk to your customers enough to know what they need and want, or you do not know enough about your business.

   There is power in the knowledge YOU have and as a business owner you should KNOW your business and all of the influencers around it. If you have control and knowledge about every facet of your business, you will know how to handle most if not all situations that happen within your business life span.

2. **There are free grants and banks that will loan individuals money if they are starting a business.**

   This is not true. You will need to contribute capital out of pocket to fund your business EVEN if you are looking for funding from other sources. Lenders, for example, will expect you to contribute at least 15-20% of your own funds (sometimes more than that) of your own funds into the business or they will automatically assume you have no faith in your business idea or that you do not have any financial responsibility or know-how.

Also, there are no truly *free grants* out there that will just give anyone funding. Most grants that do exist, which aren't many, are usually listed on www.grants.gov. These grants are usually geared towards educational institutions, nonprofits, specialized industries or emerging technologies within industries *for a reason.*

If you are the type of person that would not hand over your money to a random stranger just because they are starting their business, do not assume others will also including financial institutions. They are a business also. They cannot stay in business if they approved anyone walking through their doors asking for capital.

If you haven't found any grants you qualify for yet, it is because free grants for the general public typically do not exist and/or you do not meet the required stipulations provided by grants. Also, grants are never *free,* they always have stipulations attached and/or goals & requirements you have to achieve ahead of time before they fund your business.

3. **People will automatically love and know about your business when you officially launch.**

   This is also not true. Remember, YOUR BUSINESS is the new entity that is coming into an already <u>established</u> marketplace. It is up to you to grab the attention of consumers who are already buying similar products/services to yours from other businesses that are already in existence and convey to them in a way that they understand and like; your business exists and has better value for them.

   This isn't a *field of dreams* environment where if you build a business on a random street corner or create a website on the internet, that people will automatically trust you let alone know who you are. There are 14+ billion websites on the planet, for instance. How do you expect them to find you right away? It takes the proper marketing strategies and channels for them to hear about you and that takes time.

   The more that you can do pre-grand opening/launch marketing ...the more time you save when you do officially open.

4. **Being resistant to the notion that your original business idea and concept will change and evolve.**

   Everyone who wants to start a business, typically falls in love with the concept that they want to start. So much so, that they are resistant to change any facet of it. The problem is, consumers will only buy from a business if that business offers something that is a solution to their problems and needs.

Having a business isn't primarily about what YOU want, it is primarily about providing what potential customers want. Their purchases are what will be responsible for what hopefully keeps you in business. If you don't focus on their needs, wants and preferences – they will not buy from you and you will not have the revenue to pay your expenses. At that point, you will no longer be in business.

You will need to put the customers first and their preferences change all the time. That is how trends and technology changes. As trends change, the marketplace you are in will change and your original business concept will have to evolve to keep in step with your changing industry. If you do not change with it, you will get left behind and will ultimately have to shut down your business.

5. **There is one set magic formula for everyone who wants to start a business.**

This is definitely not true as well. Somewhere along the way in life, aspiring entrepreneurs grew up believing that there is some magical checklist in the sky that if followed, their business will be successful. This is destructive thinking.

Although there are basic business principles and a basic flow, the start-up process for every single business, including ones in the same industry, will be different. There are no predesigned processes or timelines for your business because every business and vision within each business is different. The proper strategies and operations for your business all depend on what YOU want your business to look like and then you apply the basic principles into that.

Following a pre-designed checklist or any checklist will not make you successful, being aware of business principles, the external and influencers around and in your business and having the proper strategies for your business are the minimum you will need to put your business on the right path.

These are just some of the false and risky assumptions that I see aspiring entrepreneurs and current business owners have every single day. Having these risky assumptions are what make the business owners create strategies and decisions that negatively impact a business and they are left wondering where they went wrong.

The point of the 5 assumptions I listed above (and there are a lot more to this list) is that as the business owner it is your responsibility to make the right decisions for your business and you can't be a proper business owner if you are relying on anyone other than yourself to make your business successful. You have to plan ahead of time and take the logical steps to achieve the goals you want. You have to have patience and you have to think through every situation that you encounter. You have to make time for this.

In Chapter 2, we will talk about the factors including the assumptions above that will prohibit any potential success you may have.

Chapter 2: Factors that Prohibit Success

Every year, millions of small businesses *fail* within any given year and an even higher number ***never*** get up and running for a variety of reasons:

- **In it for the wrong reasons** including trying to fix financial bad habits and personal problems and situations that have nothing to do with business.

  You will have to spend money to start and operate your business, and if you have no capital and/or you are bad with finances, you will not have the capital you need to run a business successfully.

- **Does not put in the required time, effort and capital needed for their business.**

  There is a saying in business, you will get what you give. If you put minimal effort into operating and planning strategies within your business, you will get minimal results and minimal return. You will need to make time and put money into the business constantly. You will also need to be willing to do this. This business will also need to become a priority to you, especially if it is your sole source of income.

- **Has no understanding of customer needs of the marketplace business is in.**

  The ability to stay in business will depend on the wiliness of consumers to not only purchase your products and/or services, but also that they will do it often enough that you earn enough revenue to cover your expenses plus an emergency cushion. Consumer purchases do not happen naturally – they purchase based on purpose and need. If a business provides a solution to a consumer's needs, more than likely that consumer will purchase from that particular business. It is important that you understand if your business is continuously fulfilling the needs of your customers as the constant fulfillment is the only way they will continue to purchase from your business.

  The second your business stops providing what consumers need, they will stop buying from you and may tell other people about it. As a new business, it is important for you to continue the habit of gaining consumer feedback so that you can properly evaluate how your business is doing. You need to care about what your consumers think.

- **No real differentiation in marketplace and product/service has no value offered to client.**

  It is important for your business to not only provide value to potential customers but your business needs to provide it in a way that is different from your competition and everyone else, otherwise why will they buy from you (the new guy to the market place) when there are plenty of other businesses that they are already used to. Consumers purchase based on experience, value given and word-of-mouth. As a new business, it is your job to bring something different to the marketplace **and** has to be something that consumers are not getting from other similar businesses **and** it has to be something that they care about. If you operate your business with no real value or differentiation from your competitors, consumers will make decision based on convenience, price, location and word of mouth most of all. That is a tough sell.

- **Poor management and strategy including trying to promote and sell product/service in the wrong channels and to the wrong people.**

It is virtually impossible physically and financially to sell to everyone 100% of the time, also you are going to come across 80% of the population who do not want or like the products you have to sell, and trying to convince them otherwise is a waste of your time. It is far easier to focus on the core group of people who would want to buy your products and services anyway, find where they are at and sell to them in those locations. Saves you time and saves you money. Also, it's easier to figure out what their patterns are if you only focus on a core group of people with similar lifestyles and patterns.

- **Lack of proper planning and funding to start <u>and</u> operate a business. Lack of experience, education and training in industry and/or business development & management.** If a business owner does not have the proper funds, plans, training and experience to run a business; he or she will have a tough uphill battle to climb as they will not know what they should experience from day to day nor have the capacity to handle any situations that will happen.

The goal of a business owner besides serving the needs of its customers, but it also their goal to understand the patterns within their business and industry. It is not normal to be confused daily as what you should be doing in your business. As I mentioned before, if you always find yourself confused and unsure, then you are doing something wrong.

Depending on the situation, you will need to either get more training, talk to your customers more...or research/plan/strategize your business more. Also, as I mentioned at the beginning of this guide, do not get accustomed to relying on others to make YOUR business successful. It is your business and YOU are the one responsible for it. You will have to take the self-initiative and make the proper choices in getting the training that you need.

Chapter 3: Longevity During a Down Economy

Around 2007, the economy was on a decline and as a result a lot of small businesses shut down and the unemployment rate was on the rise. This is not a new thing. Throughout history there have been many declines in the economic cycle, unemployment increases and businesses shutting down and throughout it all there have been some major corporations who were small businesses once, survive. What did they do to stay in business despite a down economy?

There are lists of hundreds of corporations that we all know including a lot that are on the Fortune 500 list that have been in business for many years that originally started as a small business during a down economy – whether at the beginning, during or at the tail end. The commonality between these lists of well-known companies is that they knew the needs of their customers at all stages. The ones who didn't, closed down.

At all stages, the business owner needs to have an ability to <u>gain insight into customer needs by engaging with them actively</u> to consistently prove the validity of their business concept and assess market potential and risks. The only way for customers to continue to purchase from your business, is only when your business continues to provide value and some benefit to them. That is the only reason why consumers buy, this fact has never changed.

You will need to implement strategies and systems within your business that will give you the ability to gain customer insight such as a mailing list, survey, basic sales conversations, etc. Point is that you must do it and you must do it often.

Chapter 4: Typical Business Start-Up Process

Although there are basic business principles in business and there is a certain flow of when you should do things based on how the different pieces of the start-up process are connected, there is no standard pre-designed check list.

But to give each of you an idea of the flow of things you should be doing in your start up process and the general connection each step has, I have included a chart below.

Keep in mind: This process is not applicable to everyone as each process is different for each business. Which steps you do and the length of time you spend each one are dependent on your specific business. Understand basic business principles and apply what's necessary for your specific business situation.

The following chapters in a good portion of this guide, we will be covering a good majority of the 1st half of the aforementioned chart and will be going into more depth on the types of actions you typically will want to make, why and how each of these steps are also interconnected with the other.

Understand each of these steps completely, will give you a better understanding of not only how business works but it will also teach you over time how to critically assess every action that is taken in your business and what the proper strategies and steps are.

Chapter 5: Preparation (Step 1)

One must be have the proper components and resources in place before they start their business. First step in starting your business is to develop your business concept by brainstorming about:

- *Your time, financial and effort capacity*

- *Required entrepreneurial traits, business management skillset and industry experience*

- *Support system – Employees, Loved Ones, Partners and Network, etc.*

Why are each of these components important?

- Provides ability to understand internal and external influencers around your business

- Provides ability to develop <u>appropriate</u> and ongoing strategies for your business that will enable you to consistently reach the target customers that are willing to purchase your product or service.

- Provides ability to figure out the answers to common questions such as:

  - Where should I sell?
  - What price should I set my products/service at?
  - Do I have enough capital?
  - What do I write in my business plan?
  - How do I attract and retain the right customers?
  - What documentation do I need to have?
  - Etc.

Time and Effort Capacity

You will not only need to have a self-starter trait but you will also need to schedule recurring time to develop and evaluate strategies with the following areas within your business:

- Management and Operations
- Legal Issues
- Human Resources
- Marketing
- Web Development and Strategy
- Accounting
- Sales, etc.

Not doing so will create gaps and problems within your business. Since you are the business owner, there is no entity above you that will remind you to do each of these tasks, so you will need to take the initiative to plan accordingly and stay on top of what is going on within your business. You need to be data driven.

Skills, Entrepreneurial Traits and Industry Experience

Having the appropriate entrepreneurial traits, business management skillset and industry experience will make owning and operating a business, less of an uphill climb and battle. It will also provide you with:

- A greater understanding of the marketplace.
- The ability to identify customers, marketing strategies and opportunities for growth.
- Greater access to a ready list of contacts for your support system and network.
- Gives you more confidence as you have a better idea of what to expect and can foresee problems more clearly.

Trusted Support System

It can be lonely at the top as a business owner and it is so easy to think that you are the only ones that are having difficulty navigating through the waters of owning and operating a business but in fact, ALL business owners have trouble most if not all of the time. It is the nature of the task. What could ease your woes is putting together a support system to be there for you emotionally or for feedback purposes every now and then so that you can analyze your business strategies.

Having a third party opinion occasionally helps you evolve mentally and helps your business grow because neutral and objective third parties can identify gaps that you cannot see in your business.

There are different types of supportive people you can have from family, friends, network, your employees, etc. Each has a role that they can play in your business growth but the key is to make sure they are the *right* people for your business such as:

- **Employees:** The individuals that you will hire to work in your business play a vital role in the brand and perception potential and current customers will have of your business. Having the right employees who care about your goals, vision and objectives will be an asset to your business. Employees who are only there to self-service their own agenda, will not care about going above and beyond and providing great customer service to your clients.

- **Business Partner(s):** Having the right business partner for your business is crucial to how well your business will do during its lifespan. When finding the appropriate business partners you will need to identify the right people who can contribute financially but also experience to your business. This can help offset any gaps in your knowledge and skillset. Keep in mind, these need to be the <u>right</u> people for your business.

  Business owners make the mistake of bringing in their family and friends as your business partner. What each of you need to remember is how they act personally, typically will be how they act in your business. One way you can protect yourself is to have a legally binding partnership agreement in place that outlines what each person is contributing, what will happen if one partner doesn't contribute equal effort, what will happen if one partner wants to leave, etc. Each of you cannot get hung up in the assumed glamour and fame and really need to talk about the operational pieces of the business before you launch. Time and time again I have seen businesses fail because there is a dysfunction between the business partners of the business.

- **Network:** You will need to put together a network of professionals in your industry or an advisory board that will be able to give you their unbiased and objective opinion on the strategies within your business. You can develop a network of people through contacts you meet within your industry, people you meet at Trade Association or Chambers of Commerce events. Point is, you cannot do this on your own and you do need industry opinions on things that you do and would like to do in your business.

- **Loved Ones:** Before you begin the process of starting your business, your family needs to be on board and be okay with you being gone more often than you use to. At times, your business will be more important and more of a priority than your business and they will have to be okay with that. Talk about possible scenarios with your spouse and other loved ones so they truly understand how important having this business will mean to you.

Chapter 6: Conceptualization and Research (Step 2)

Is this a business or a hobby?

After you have thoroughly investigated your preparedness emotionally, physically, time and willingness you will have to start defining the business idea in a more concrete fashion. Occasionally, an individual (this tends to happen in certain industries such as food based and creative backgrounds) gets told that what that should utilize their talents and start a business. Part of the problem with situations such as this and especially for those with artsy, creative or textile type of backgrounds. Typically individuals from these backgrounds have talents, sometimes it is not enough to have a sustainable business due to the fact that there isn't enough demand or potential customers will not purchase often enough for someone to cover expenses that will occur monthly.

There are several tests that one can use to really evaluate if their business idea is more of a hobby or if it has the potential to be a thriving and sustainable business. Some self-test questions you can ask yourself are:

- Is there <u>enough</u> of a market for it to build a sustainable income?

- Is the product/service a want or is it a need (solution to a problem)?

- Can it generate a profit?

- Is it scalable?

Creating a Business Concept

When you have a business idea, your goal in the very beginning is to develop it enough for you to have enough information to research its viability. You need to brainstorm and be aware of your products/service, competitors, target market, pricing, distribution channels and support system. Let's take a look at each of these components of a proper business concept below:

1. **The product or service(s) being offered including identifying features and end user benefits of each.**

    - Every single product or service should be a solution to a problem, fulfill a need or improve an existing solution not based on simply a want. Sustainability cannot exist without true value offered that exists beyond wants and features.

    - Start by listing and describing each of your products or services i.e. attributes and know what purpose each item serves in solving a target customer's needs. How will it create value for them and how do they benefit?

- Remember, customers only buy products for **end user benefits** of product/service features and not the features itself!

- Think about all of the smart phones out there, especially the most popular one. You know which one I am referring to but in thinking about this particular brand and all of its reoccurring customers, what is perceived as? Think beyond functionality:

  f. Personal Assistant/Organizer
  g. Device that keeps you connected with loved ones
  h. Fitting In/Ego
  i. Other
  j. All of the above

The answer is **C. Fitting In / Ego**. The reasoning behind this answer is there are hundreds of smart phone brands out there that can do the same things: be a personal assistant/organizer, allows you to call/email/text loved ones, etc. but the difference between these brands and the most popular brand is that the 14-25 year old target market (core group of customers) buy based on what is most popular in itself because they themselves want to belong.

2. The identified target market(s) of your business

When it comes to brainstorming about your business concept you will also have to brainstorm about your identified target market, you need to start by thinking about who is most likely to buy what you have to sell.   For example, think about the following scenario:

Two 30 year old women, both living in an upper class neighborhood with the same income, education, ethnicity but two different lifestyles: Soccer Mom vs. Business Professional.

When it comes to most products that they will purchase, will they acquire the same things around the same days, times, hours and quantities? More likely not. Although both women have similar profiles, their lifestyles are different. Lifestyles impact when they do things, what they are interested in and what their priorities are so as a business owner we can assume we can target and sell to everyone because it is physically and financially impossible to do so.

So instead of trying to assume the entire population will be interested in what you have to sell, it is far easier to figure out who would naturally be interested in the types of things you have to sell, understand their characteristics and where there typically are at, and communicate with them in ways they understand. This is far easier than trying to convince people to buy from you.

The **SOLE** existence of your business is to provide your core group of customers with the products/services they need, at the price they expect in the areas/times that they want.

REMEMBER the 80/20 Rule:
"20% of customers contribute to 80% of your sales"
(target customers)

The second goal of your business is to service your core group of customers (target market) well enough so that they become loyal customers. Loyal customers are very important because they are:

- Less sensitive to price changes
- They provide word-of-mouth and referrals
- Likely to purchase multiple or supplemental products/services
- Require less educating and selling time
- Makes your job easier and more satisfying

To create a profile of your potential target market, start by focusing on the core group of customers that will comprise most of your sales (**target customers**) and what you need to know about them:

- Their demographics and psychographics
- How they would typically use your product/service
- What influences their buying behaviors and purchasing patterns
- *What do they value?* Is it the features/benefits that you listed about your product/service? This requires speaking with potential customers to gather their insight and preferences.

Knowing these facts about your potential target market will enable you to better shape your business strategies and operations in meeting their needs. It will also help shape your elevator pitch and messaging on all of your marketing material and website.

3. Potential competitors and their strengths/weaknesses

All business regardless of how unique they are have competitors. Both direct and indirect. **Direct competitors** are businesses that operate similarly to you while **indirect competitors** are businesses that operate as an alternative to you.

When analyzing your competitors, at the very minimum you will need to find out things such as:

- Who are your competitors? Know at least 5 (a mix of indirect/direct)
- What are their products/services and how do they communicate the value of each?
- How do they promote and brand their business?
- Who are their target market(s)?
- How do they price their products/services?
- What are their revenue streams (distribution channels)?
- What their customers think about them and how you can capitalize on it

4. Appropriate distribution channel(s)

When identifying where you will earn your revenue (also known as revenue streams/distribution channels) you need to identify the appropriate places that your target market that you had profiled earlier can be found. It makes no sense to try and sell and market at locations where your target market will never be. Possible distribution channels are:

- Brick and Mortar
- Online / E-Commerce
- Mobile
- Farmer's Market
- Consignment
- Other retailers
- Sales Reps
- Others
- All of the above

The key to this is remember if your identified target market(s) can be found in those places and also if it is cost effective to do so.

5. A pricing strategy

You will need to figure out how to price your product or service. It is simply not enough to price without any logical reason why and it is just as bad to price just based on what your competitors are charging. You cannot price exactly the same as others because your business is different and your costs to operate is different. When pricing, you should consider factors such as:

- Generating enough revenue to create a profit. **This requires doing financial projections.**

- The value of your product/service i.e. expertise, delivery convenience, location, etc. **This requires knowing your product/service and what**

the unique selling proposition and value proposition is.

- The criteria target customers use to make purchasing decisions. **This requires talking to them.**
- Competitors rates unless there is a strong differentiation then it should be comparable. **This requires performing a competitor analysis.**

6. Key partners and support system with outlined contributions

Do you have people in your life that will work with you, work for you, give you their industry perspective and support your decisions and time away? Ideally you will want to bring people into your business that are the right people who share the same vision and work ethic as you do. You also need to outline their contributions to your business on paper and hold them accountable for it. If they have actions that hurt your business, you will need to let them go.

Market Research // Feasibility (Viability Study)

After you have defined your business idea in a more concrete way, take the time to do thorough research to find out if your business idea will fit into the already established marketplace for your industry and product/service. If you find that your idea will not fit into the marketplace, do not proceed forward. You need to solve the hindrances that will cause your business idea to not operate successfully.

How and what you research depend on the questions YOU are looking for the answers to. Think about what it is you need to know to be fully confident that your idea will fit (or logically improve) and compete but not go against it and WHY. This is called a feasibility analysis.

Research can be direct research you perform yourself or data you collect from research performed by someone else. You can conduct research and analyze data through avenues such as:

- Surveys and focus groups you implement with your target market profile
- Market research companies (paid & fee based)
- Trade Journals and Associations
- Chambers of Commerce
- Tradeshows and Expos for your industry
- Research Databases (paid & fee based)
- Etc.

Chapter 7: Business Planning and Projections (Step 3)

It is highly recommended that you do not try and write a business plan if you have not developed a solid business concept and performed the necessary research you need to determine if your business idea will be feasible or not as mentioned in previous chapters.

There is no purpose in writing a plan for a business that is not feasible and will not do well. In this chapter, we will be going over briefly the purpose of a business plan and what it consists of. If you need a more thorough explanation of what a business plan entails feel free and check out my other book: Small Business How To Guide to Writing a Business Plans Easily.

Although, writing a business plan is not a *must do*, but it is an integral part of the business start-up process. You should not write a business plan because you think you have to, write a business plan because you KNOW you NEED to and why. There has to be a reason why you want to write it, or it will be ineffective to your business. There are two main purposes why most people want to write a business plan: Internal and External.

Internal Purposes

- Internal roadmap of your business outlining what your vision for the business is, what you would like to do and how you plan on achieving your vision.
- Greater understanding of what you are doing within business through
- Increase likelihood of success

External Purposes

- Needed if trying to obtain financing.
- May be requested by third parties other than lenders
- Potential partners or collaborators

What is in a business plan?

- **Executive Summary** (First in plan but written last)
- **Business Description and Vision** – Company Background, history goals, objectives, mission and vision
- **Products and Services** – list of products/services, features, benefits, value added, pricing
- **Organization and Management** – management team, qualifications, special certifications
- **Marketing** – Industry trends, marketplace data, strategy of how your business will compete, target market, competitor analysis, etc.

- **Operating Plan** – location information, parking requirements, zoning, processes, systems etc.
- **Financial Information** – financial projections, costs, financial statements, sales forecasted, etc.

Why Write a Business Plan?

What you put into the plan is a description of the business YOU are wanting to create. Because your business plan is about the business you are trying to start and operate, it is not advisable to have a 3rd party write it as they do not know what it is YOU want to do and how YOU want to do it.

All of the required sections are pretty straightforward and are all items you need to think about and decide on. If you find yourself lost when writing a business plan, it is because you have not thought through your business concept thoroughly. Go back and further conceptualize your business idea as the different components of a developed business concept are similar to <u>most</u> of the sections of a business plan:

<u>Business Concept Components</u>	<u>Business Plan Sections</u>
Product Service ⟶	Products and Services
Target Market ⟶	Marketing
Competitor Analysis ⟶	Marketing
Pricing Strategy ⟶	Product and Services/Marketing
Distribution Channels ⟶	Marketing/Operational Plan
Cost Analysis ⟶	Financial Plan
Sales Forecast ⟶	Financial Plan
Key Partners and Support System ⟶	Organization & Management

How much will it cost to start and operate your business?

The startup and operational costs you may encounter depending on the nature of your business and what YOU want it to look like. Every business is different and thus the costs of every business and even ones in the same industry will be different.

When projecting your start up and operational costs make sure you factor in how it affects how much you can <u>realistically earn.</u> Good idea is to overestimate your expenses and underestimate your revenue. Always plan for worst case scenario.

Start- Up Costs include: Licenses/Permits, TI, Marketing, Equipment, Vehicles, Furniture, Utility Deposits, Merchant Services, Employee costs, insurance, professional fees, etc.

Operational Costs

- **Fixed Costs include:** Supplies, Utilities, Rent, Marketing/Advertising, etc.
- **Variable Costs include:** Costs that you incur in order to make & sell goods or provide a service i.e. ingredients, mileage etc.

> **Know your breakeven point!**
> Break-even point = fixed costs / (unit selling price - variable

Chapter 8: Identifying Funding Options (Step 4)

Do you have enough capital?

It is imperative that you have sufficient capital to not only start your business but also to maintain it. It isn't until you project your costs, will you know if you currently have enough funds out of pocket to make your business idea happen. There are several options if you do not have sufficient capital out of pocket. Obviously, the best choice would be to save until you can pay for most of your start up and operational expenses out of pocket to eliminate a lot of unnecessary debt in the beginning but we all know especially since the economic decline in 2007/2008 that is very difficult these days.

There are various types of financing and we will talk about the most common ones in this chapter:

Debt Financing

Debt financing is obtaining capital such as loans without giving up equity or ownership in the business to obtain it. Debt financing can come from financial institutions, lending institutions, non-traditional lenders.

The lending requirements vary between lending institutions and as mentioned in the beginning of this book, they do not give you money just because you are starting a business or because you are Mr. Nice Guy or Gal. They are a business themselves and one of the way earn revenue and stay in business is a client's ability to pay back the capital they borrowed plus the agreed upon interest.

Because lending institutions are dependent on a client's ability to pay, they implement qualification thresholds to eliminate a lot of the risks in lending. Typical lending considerations although vary between place to place, they all have typical minimums between all of them which are dependent on the capital amount you are requesting and other requirements. They will evaluate you based on the financial documents you submit as part of your loan application. The typical documents they will assess are:

- **Satisfactory FICO Score and Credit History**. Scores they typically have accepted were at minimums of 680-720 or higher. Some institutions have accepted lower credit scores of around 650 but it was more likely due to the individuals other financial documents surpassed the institution's expectations.

- **3 Years of most recent tax returns**. This is how they evaluate your income level interests to determine that if you had to return to the workforce, would your expected salary be sufficient to pay back a loan for the capital amount you want to request.

- **Collateral** – The higher capital amount you are requesting, the more they will expect you to have assets that are a 1 to 1 match in value. For example, if you are seeking $200K or more in capital, they will definitely expect you to have home equity of equal amount. The purpose is the financial institutions want their money back ASAP and if you default, they want to be able to liquidate assets you have quickly to get it.

- **Industry Experience** and **Business Plan.** They typically ask for your resume to show your industry experience as well as your business plan. These two sets of documents provide them with the opportunity to see if you have experience in the industry you would like to start a business in and do you have strong plan in place to make this business successful.

- Can contribute at least **25-30% out-of-pocket.** This is a set in stone standard for most financial institutions. This also helps them see that you have faith in your business idea.

- **Industry and growth trends.** They will look into the industry and see if it is a growing, declining or stagnant market. Sometimes the approval process isn't about you and your talents and plans, sometimes they will not approve someone because the industry they are getting into is declining and that scares financial institutions.

- **Written explanation** of amount seeking and a **breakdown of associated costs.** Financial institutions will often request a written statement of the amount you are seeking plus a breakdown of what you would like to use the funds for and any associate costs. They want to see what you will do with funds or if it was you just picking a number out of thin air.

Personal Financing

- Out-of-pocket: Minimum of 25-30%
- Family/Friends

Equity Financing

- Trusted Business Partner with capital to contribute
- Investor

Other

- Crowdfunding is a viable option dependent on the type of business you would like to start. Most business owners who use crowdfunding to fund their business and are unsuccessful at it is typically because they assume that they can just design a campaign without promoting it. Like the internet, there are millions of people on crowdfunding sites, so how will people find you if you do not talk about it or promote your campaign.

- Scale down/start small to where it fits your financial means is the most logical step if you cannot get outside funding for your business. There is nothing wrong with starting your business on a smaller scale so you don't incur any unnecessary expenses from the start. This also is a true benefit to people with minimal industry experience as starting small is less of a risk to obtain that experience. If an aspiring entrepreneur can make their concept work on a smaller scale, then they can grow into their ideal scenario instead of starting big and failing and most often times, not being able to adjust to the failure or adapt to it.

- *Free Grants?* As mentioned in the beginning of this guide, although there are free grants out there on legitimate sites such as www.grants.gov , very rarely if at all are these grants designed for the general public. Grants are made available because an economic development agency or governmental institution whether its federal, state or local has tasks within the community they need to solve and will occasionally recruit businesses to help them solve those economic issues. Thus grants are offered as a way to bring those specific businesses they need to solve those issues.

  For example, a hair salon very rarely will qualify for a grant because most salons don't solve an economic need.

Chapter 9: What's Next?

After viability has been evaluated, next step would be to start the planning process i.e. developing a business plan to outline strategies to be used to launch business concept as described in previous chapters.

What makes a business feasible and viable is a business that has **the proper people, funding, business concept, plan and strategies in place before it starts.**

Without all of these things, you will not start off in the right direction and gaps will occur. If gaps and problems occur, be aware that it can snowball quickly and will require a strong financial capacity in order to fix it. More than likely if problems have snowballed, the business owner more than likely does not have financial capacity to fix it at any rate.

Chapter 10: Business Development (Stage 5)

By now you have learned about what the small business landscape is like, how to prepare yourself, how to develop a business concept, obtaining funding, writing a business plan and maybe after all of that, the concept doesn't work no matter what you do. Sometimes it's not the concept itself but the avenue to which you start it.

Besides starting a small business independently, depending on your situation there may be more viable options to start your business in order to make it work. Other options besides starting an independent business are buying an existing independent business or buying a franchise.

Starting an Independent Business

This is the most common option but it can be the most risky. It is the most risky because you are essentially starting a business from scratch. But this also can be an advantage because you have the ability to create a business from the ground up according to what you envision.

Always be aware of the time, effort and financial requirements of having to create a proof of concept when consumers do not know your business exists and do not know who you are. There is no existing loyalty or trust. You should not fall victim to the field of dreams misconception to where if you build a business, automatically thinking they will come and purchase.

Independent businesses can have various set ups including brick & mortar, online, mobile, shared space, farmer's market, etc. It is much easier to deal with starting small and within your means, than to overshoot and fail.

Buying an Existing Business

The other avenue you pursue is buying an existing business especially if you aren't the creative and macro level thinker. When purchasing an existing business it gives you ownership of an existing product and/or service, the existing client base, existing suppliers and existing employees if applicable.

When buying an existing business, beware of the fact that the previous owners may not be entirely forthcoming about any operational and financial issues or that it may contain ineffective employees that you personally wouldn't hire or a tremendous amount of dissatisfied customers.

If you want to go this route, then be sure to do your research and be thorough in evaluating if their selling price is sufficient for what you will potentially be getting into.

Buying a Franchise

Buying an existing franchise is a lot like buying an existing independent business except the difference is that a franchise has a proven formula that you will have to follow. An existing independent business more than likely will just give you the clients and the equipment and maybe marketing materials, but very rarely they will give you the working formula to make it happen.

This is the bonus of a franchise. A franchise is designed to give you the formula for you to follow and most of the time if not all of the time the franchisor does not want you to deter from that.

They typically will charge you a set franchise fee to purchase the franchise location and it gives you the right to use the name of an established proof of concept and the ability to sell its products and/or services. The franchisor will also typically will charge you a royalty fee (typically between 3-12% of sales) on a recurring basis for continued support and the right to continue using the name.

The franchisor also typically dictates fees, locations to choose from, what they will provide you, what vendors you must buy your inventory from and what you can do within the business.

It is best if going the franchise route to pick a franchise that best fits your style and industry experience because the purchase does not automatically guarantee success and growth. It is up to you and your knowledge and efforts to maintain the formula the franchisor has designed to make the franchise successful.

Take away

The #1 question that all aspiring entrepreneurs ask is **How Do I Start My Business?** The answer is it depends on you. Having a business means that you as the owner are essentially dictating how the business starts and how it will operate and also as the owner you are the only person responsible for finding the right strategy to make it work. You can ask and research all you want, but you are the one that has to apply all of these principles to your specific business situation.

Before you decide to start your business and launch it, you should ask yourself several questions:

- Are you prepared?

- Do you have all the right resources and people in place?

- Do you know the industry and environment around your business?

- Do you have enough funding to start and operate your business?

- Do you have the right strategies to reach the core group of people who would be interested in my product/service?

If the answers to any or all of these questions are **no**, then you haven't prepared enough and you are not ready to launch. The more that you prepare ahead of time before obtaining sufficient documentation, marketing materials and incurring any expenses the less risks you will start with.

THE END.

I wanted to thank all of you for taking the time to read this starting a business guide. I do hope it gave you a clear explanation of the proper way to prepare yourself as a new entrepreneur, what the typical start up process is, how to write a business plan, understanding the lending process, what goes in it and most of all what you are supposed to do each relevant section about your business.

I hope you have enjoyed the book and if you could take the time and review the book. Reviews help me become aware of what you enjoyed and didn't enjoy within the book and what you would like for me to improve. It also will help me find out about what other information you will want to know in the future.

For those of you who want to review the book, you can do so by clicking here.

Thank you.

For those of you who purchased this book because you also wanted free access to the **bonus books**, please click here to access it for free now!

If you would like to subscribe to the ***Starting a Business by Susan Monthly Tips and Tricks*** newsletter for **FREE** information about how to start, grow and operate your business more successful, you can subscribe and opt-in here.

Want more?

Phew! You made it through the basic process of Starting a Business and more depth about the Business Planning process that you read in the bonus book.

I'm very grateful that you took the time to read this, so I wanted to give you some bonus material.

I've taught hundreds among hundreds of people how to not only create a strong business concept but also the step by step process to starting a business so that they can not only do things that they love but also earn a stable income doing it.

If you want free access to my bonus material including a business plan template and a template to figure out your startup costs, make sure to sign up for my email list, where you can get the templates sent to you right away.

You can get the templates by signing up here.

Susan Kilmer
Founder of Business by Susan